The Domestic Violence Survival Workbook

Self-Assessments, Exercises
& Educational Handouts

John J. Liptak, EdD
Ester A. Leutenberg

Illustrated by
Amy L. Brodsky, LISW

wholeperson
Stress & Wellness Publishers

101 W. 2nd St., Suite 203
Duluth, MN 55802

800-247-6789

books@wholeperson.com
www.wholeperson.com

The Domestic Violence Survival Workbook
Self-Assessments, Exercises & Educational Handouts

Printed in the United States of America

10 9 8 7 6 5 4 3 2

Editorial Director: Carlene Sippola
Art Director: Joy Morgan Dey

Library of Congress Control Number: 2008942358
ISBN: 978-1-57025-231-0

Using This Book *(For the professional)*

Over the past few decades the problems of family violence and domestic abuse have been brought to the forefront of our consciousness. The reality is that domestic violence occurs in families of all races, cultures, and socio-economic levels. Recognizing early warning signs is critical in the reduction of domestic violence. Part of the problem is that domestic violence encompasses many different types of abuse:

- **Physical abuse** includes slapping, hitting, punching, shoving, kicking, choking, pushing, grabbing, pulling hair, depriving of food, light and/or water, and many other ways of physically harming another person. Sometimes physical abuse involves being hit with a weapon or an object, or even left alone in dangerous places or tied up and left for periods of time.

- **Sexual abuse** is when a partner is forced to participate in sexual situations against his or her will. This can include sexual intercourse when the partner is not fully conscious, has not given consent, or is afraid to say no. This might also include sexual situations in which one partner coerces the other to engage in sexual activities that are not mutually agreed upon.

- **Psychological, emotional or verbal abuse** is when one partner threatens, humiliates, excessively blames, puts-down, intimidates or otherwise psychologically hurts the other partner. This may include situations in which a partner is made to feel inferior, stupid or lazy. This type of abuse can also take the form of one partner depriving the other of things they need or keeping them away from other people.

- **Financial abuse** occurs when a partner takes financial advantage by cashing checks without permission, taking money and personal belongings, forging a partner's signature, lying about how much money they have, or using deception, scare tactics, trickery or false pretense for financial gain.

- **Multiple forms of abuse** are when one partner abuses the other partner in more than one of the ways listed.

Professionals agree that domestic violence is very complex and can take many different forms. Abusers can include spouses, boyfriends and girlfriends, same-sex partners, roommates and friends. It may appear that the obvious and simple solution to this problem is that a domestic violence survivor should just leave the abuser and the abusive relationship. Many reasons exist to indicate why this is not always possible or desirable on the part of the abused. The good news is that skills for recognizing and effectively dealing with abusive relationships can be learned.

Over the last century many different workbooks, workshops and self-help systems have been designed to help people explore ways of overcoming abusive relationships. In the past twenty years, many research studies have focused on the value of self-reflection and journaling as a way of exploring personal characteristics, identifying ineffective behaviors, and examining thoughts and feelings that lead to these ineffective behaviors. This book is unique in that it combines two powerful psychological tools designed to enhance domestic violence coping skills: self-assessment and journaling.

Using This Book *(For the professional, continued)*

Different cultures construct relationships and gender in different ways, For example, some cultures expect relationships to include more possessiveness and even a healthy relationship may score high on the Scales. This does not always indicate a higher incidence of abuse in this community. While the book attempts to be inter-culturally relevant and sensitive, therapists and other professionals must use discretion, sensitivity and cultural competency in their use of these materials.

The *Domestic Violence Survival Workbook* contains five separate sections that will help participants learn more about themselves as well as the impact of domestic violence in their lives and the lives of their family members. The five sections of this book are:

- **SYMPTOMS OF ABUSE SCALE** helps survivors to explore the extent to which abuse is having on their physical wellness, emotions, thought patterns and detachment from others.

- **TYPES of ABUSE SCALE** helps survivors explore and examine their relationship with parents, siblings, grandparents, children, friends and work colleagues. *It includes a comprehensive 10-page safety plan. Please stress the comments in the bottom box of each page on how to keep the Safety Plan SAFE!*

- **PARTNER BEHAVIOR SCALE** helps individuals identify if they are in a potentially abusive relationship.

- **ELDER ABUSE SCALE** helps survivors of elder abuse explore, examine and manage a variety of emotions.

- **SELF-EMPOWERMENT SCALE** helps survivors examine if they are successfully moving on from the trauma of abuse and living the life they have dreamed of living.

These sections serve as avenues for individual self-reflection, as well as for group experiences revolving around identified topics of importance. Each assessment includes directions for easy administration, scoring and interpretation. Each section includes exploratory activities, reflective journaling activities and educational handouts to help participants discover their habitual, ineffective methods of managing domestic violence and exploring new ways to bring about healing.

The art of self-reflection goes back many centuries and is rooted in many of the world's greatest spiritual and philosophical traditions. Socrates, the ancient Greek philosopher, was known to walk the streets engaging the people he met in philosophical reflection and dialogue. He felt that this type of activity was so important in life that he went so far as to proclaim, "The unexamined life is not worth living!" The unexamined life is one in which the same routine is continually repeated without ever thinking about its meaning to one's life and how this life really could be lived. However, a structured reflection and examination of beliefs, assumptions, characteristics, and patterns can provide a better understanding, which can lead to a more satisfying life. A greater level of self-understanding about important life skills is often necessary to make positive, self-directed changes in the negative patterns that keep repeating throughout life. The assessments and exercises in this book can help promote this self-understanding. Through involvement in the in-depth activities, the participant claims ownership in the development of positive patterns.

Journaling is an extremely powerful tool for enhancing self-discovery, learning, transcending traditional problems, breaking ineffective life habits, and helping to heal from psychological traumas of the past. From a physical point of view, writing reduces stress and lowers muscle tension, blood pressure and heart rate levels. Psychologically, writing reduces sadness, depression and general anxiety, and leads to a greater level of life satisfaction and optimism. Behaviorally, writing leads to enhanced social skills, emotional intelligence and creativity. It also leads to improved writing skills which leads to more self-confidence in the workplace.

By combining reflective assessment and journaling, your participants will be exposed to a powerful method of combining verbalizing and writing to reflect and solve problems, becoming more aware of domestic violence in their lives.

Preparation for using the assessments and activities in this book is important. The authors suggest that prior to administering any of the assessments in this book, you complete them yourself. This will familiarize you with the format of the assessments, the scoring directions, the interpretation guides and the journaling activities. Although the assessments are designed to be self-administered, scored and interpreted, it helps for facilitators to be prepared to answer questions about the assessments for participants.

With your background and experience, as well as familiarity with the scales, you should be able to clarify for participants any confusing words or phrases.

The Assessments, Journaling Activities and Educational Handouts

The Assessments, Journaling Activities, and Educational Handouts in *The Domestic Violence Survival Workbook* are reproducible and ready to be photocopied for participants' use. Assessments contained in this book focus on self-reported data and are similar to ones used by psychologists, counselors, therapists and career consultants. Accuracy and usefulness of the information provided is dependent on the truthful information that each participant provides through self-examination. By being honest, participants help themselves to learn about unproductive and ineffective patterns, and to uncover information that might be keeping them from being as happy and/or as successful as they might be.

An assessment instrument can provide participants with valuable information about themselves; however, it cannot measure or identify everything about them. The purposes of the assessments are not to pigeon-hole certain characteristics, but rather to allow participants to explore all of their characteristics. This book contains self-assessments, not tests. Tests measure knowledge or whether something is right or wrong. For the assessments in this book, there are no right or wrong answers. These assessments ask for personal opinions or attitudes about a topic of importance in the participant's career and life.

When administering assessments in this workbook, remember that the items are generically written so that they will be applicable to a wide variety of people but will not account for every possible variable for every person. The assessments are not specifically tailored to one person. Use them to help participants identify negative themes in their lives and find ways to break the hold that these patterns and their effects have.

Advise the participants taking the assessments that they should not spend too much time trying to analyze the content of the questions; their initial response will most likely be true. Regardless of individual scores, encourage participants to talk about their findings and their feelings pertaining to what they have discovered about themselves. Talking about abusive patterns and relationships can enhance the life of participants. These domestic violence exercises can be used by group facilitators working with either potential victims of domestic violence or past or present survivors of domestic violence.

A particular score on any assessment does not guarantee a participant's level of safety or danger in a relationship. Use discretion when using any of the information or feedback provided in this workbook. The use of these assessments should not be substituted for consultation and/or safety planning with a domestic violence professional. Should the participants experience any emotional, mental, or physical problems, they need to consult a qualified mental health care professional.

Thanks to the following professionals whose input in this book has been so valuable!

Carol Butler, MS Ed, RN, C, Nancy Day, OT Reg (Ont), Eileen Regen, M.Ed., CJE

Special thanks to Kerry Moles, CSW and Shayna Livia Korb, BS for their expertise on the crucial topic of Domestic Violence.

Without their thought-provoking questions and professional insights, this book would not have been possible.

Layout of the Book

The Domestic Violence Survival Workbook is designed to be used either independently or as part of an integrated curriculum. You may administer one of the assessments and the journaling exercises to an individual or a group with whom you are working, or you may administer a number of the assessments over one or more days.

This book includes five sections, each of which contains:

- **Assessment Instruments** – Self-assessment inventories with scoring directions and interpretation materials. Group facilitators can choose one or more of the activities relevant to their participants.

- **Activity Handouts** – Practical questions and activities that prompt self-reflection and promote self-understanding. These questions and activities foster introspection and promote pro-social behaviors.

- **Reflective Questions for Journaling** – Self-exploration activities and journaling exercises specific to each assessment to enhance self-discovery, learning and healing.

- **Educational Handouts** – Handouts designed to enhance instruction can be used individually or in groups to enhance awareness of abuse and abusive relationships. They can be distributed, converted into masters for overheads or transparencies, or written down on a board and discussed.

Who should use this program?

This book has been designed as a practical tool for helping professionals, such as therapists, counselors, psychologists, teachers, group leaders, etc. Depending on the role of the professional using *The Domestic Violence Survival Workbook* and the specific group's needs, these sections can be used individually, combined, or as part of an integrated curriculum for a more comprehensive approach.

Why use self-assessments?

Self-assessments are important in teaching various domestic violence survival skills. Participants will:

- Become aware of the primary motivators that guide their behavior.

- Explore and learn to indentify situations that are potentially harmful.

- Explore the effects of unconscious childhood messages.

- Gain insight that will guide behavioral change.

- Focus their thinking on behavioral goals for change.

- Uncover resources they possess that can help them to cope with problems and difficulties.

- Explore their personal characteristics without judgment.

- Develop full awareness of their strengths and weaknesses.

Because the assessments are presented in a straightforward and easy-to-use format, individuals can self-administer, score, and interpret each assessment at their own pace.

Introduction for the Participant

Domestic violence is the number one cause of injury to women and men in the United States. Domestic violence is a crime that cuts across all racial, cultural, age and socio-economic lines. Violence at home between partners can take many forms including physical, sexual, financial, verbal and emotional abuse. Most men and women who abuse their partners tended to witness violence in their own family as they were growing up or were abused as children.

People who have been abused often believe they somehow cause the abuse, or that they can control the abuse by pleasing his or her partner or not causing him or her to get angry. If you are one of those people, you probably are still exhibiting a variety of symptoms that disrupt your life, your relationship with others, your work, and your family interactions. Some of the thoughts, feelings and behaviors of abuse survivors include:

- Low self-esteem
- Controlling behaviors
- Lack of trust
- Anxiety
- Guilt about being responsible for the abuse
- Fear of abandonment

The good news is that if you are possibly about to be abused by someone, being abused now, or have been abused in the past, this book can help you! Many abusers are not even aware of the patterns and triggers for their abusive actions. On the other hand, many people being abused find themselves caught up in a cycle of abuse that follows a common pattern in their relationships.

This book relies on assessments and journaling activities to help you reflect on yourself and your relationships. This method is both educational and therapeutic. *The Domestic Violence Survival Workbook* is designed to help you learn about the types of abuse, how to take better care of yourself, and how to identify abusive personality characteristics.

Many people who were abused go on to abuse others.

If you have concerns about this issue, please call the National Domestic Violence Hotline at 1-800-799-7233.

The Domestic Violence Survival Workbook
TABLE OF CONTENTS

TABLE OF CONTENTS *(continued)*

SECTION III – Partner Behavior

Partner Behavior Scale

Activity Handouts

TABLE OF CONTENTS *(continued)*

TABLE OF CONTENTS *(continued)*

SECTION I:
Symptoms of Abuse Scale

Name_____

Date_____

Symptoms of Abuse Scale Directions

Domestic violence is a pattern of behavior in an intimate relationship that is used to obtain and maintain power and control over an intimate partner. Stress is often the result of this abuse. The Symptoms of Abuse Scale is designed to help you explore different types of symptoms that you may be experiencing that are related to stress.

This booklet contains statements that are divided into four categories. Read each of the statements and decide how descriptive the statement is of you. In each of the choices listed, circle the number of your response on the line to the right of each statement.

In the following example, the circled 1 indicates that the statement is not at all descriptive of the person completing the inventory:

	A Lot Like Me	Somewhat Like Me	A Little Like Me	Not Like Me
I. I find that . . .				
I feel detached from other people around me	4	3	2	(1)

This is not a test and there are no right or wrong answers. Do not spend too much time thinking about your answers. Your initial response will be the most true for you. Be sure to respond to every statement.

(Turn to the next page and begin)

Symptoms of Abuse Scale

	A Lot Like Me	Somewhat Like Me	A Little Like Me	Not Like Me
I. I find that . . .				
I feel detached from other people around me	4	3	2	1
I have lost interest in important social activities	4	3	2	1
I have lost interest in my job	4	3	2	1
I have lost interest in hobbies and sports	4	3	2	1
I avoid activities or places that remind me of the abuse	4	3	2	1
I avoid people or conversations that remind me of the abuse	4	3	2	1
I have difficulty being around my friends	4	3	2	1
I try to avoid feelings that remind me of the abuse	4	3	2	1

DETACHED TOTAL = _____

	A Lot Like Me	Somewhat Like Me	A Little Like Me	Not Like Me
II. I find that . . .				
I have frequent headaches	4	3	2	1
I am jumpy if startled by sudden noises	4	3	2	1
I have recurring panic attacks	4	3	2	1
I often have an upset stomach	4	3	2	1
I am experiencing a decrease or increase of appetite	4	3	2	1
I am tired a lot of the time	4	3	2	1
I frequently have a dry mouth or throat	4	3	2	1
I often feel anxious	4	3	2	1

PHYSICAL SYMPTOMS TOTAL = _____

(Continued on the next page)

(Symptoms of Abuse Scale, continued)

	A Lot Like Me	Somewhat Like Me	A Little Like Me	Not Like Me
III. I find that . . .				
I think about the abuse a lot of the time	4	3	2	1
I get mental pictures of the abuse without being reminded of it	4	3	2	1
I am unable to remember parts of the abuse	4	3	2	1
I am unable to remember my life during the abuse	4	3	2	1
I have sudden flashbacks of the abuse	4	3	2	1
I have difficulty falling asleep	4	3	2	1
I relive the abuse in my mind	4	3	2	1
I have a hard time concentrating	4	3	2	1

COGNITIVE TOTAL = _____

	A Lot Like Me	Somewhat Like Me	A Little Like Me	Not Like Me
IV. I find that . . .				
I feel numb emotionally	4	3	2	1
I feel guilty about the abuse	4	3	2	1
I have bad dreams and nightmares	4	3	2	1
I get emotionally upset when I think about the abuse	4	3	2	1
I don't know who to trust	4	3	2	1
I am on guard most of the time	4	3	2	1
I am irritable a lot of the time	4	3	2	1
I have feelings of hopelessness	4	3	2	1

EMOTIONS TOTAL = _____

(Go to the Scoring Directions on the next page)

Symptoms of Abuse Scale Scoring Directions

The Symptoms of Abuse Scale is designed to measure the severity and the nature of the symptoms of the abuse you are currently experiencing. For each of the four sections on the previous pages, count the scores you circled for each of the eight items. Put that total on the line marked "Total" at the end of each section.

Then, transfer your totals to the spaces below:

I.   DETACHED TOTAL   =   _____

II. PHYSICAL SYMPTOMS TOTAL   =   _____

III. COGNITIVE TOTAL   =   _____

IV. EMOTIONS TOTAL   =   _____

Profile Interpretation

TOTAL SCALES SCORES	RESULT	INDICATIONS
Scores from 25 to 32	High	You have many of the symptoms of extreme stress. You need to do much more to eliminate some of the stress in your life.
Scores from 16 to 24	Moderate	You have some of the symptoms of extreme stress. You need to do more to eliminate some of the stress in your life.
Scores from 8 to 15	Low	You may not have any or you may have a few of the symptoms of extreme stress. You may not need to do anything if you have a very low score, or it may help you to do a little to eliminate some stress in your life.

For scales which you scored in the **Moderate** or **High** range, find the descriptions on the pages that follow. Read the description and complete the exercises that are included. No matter how you scored, low, moderate or high, you will benefit from these exercises.

Symptoms of Abuse Scale
Profile Interpretation *(Continued)*

I. DETACHED

People who are experiencing extreme stress are often detached and have lost interest in life. You possibly have lost interest in activities that are important to you like your job, school, hobbies, sports, house-of-worship or spiritual activities and/or social activities. You may feel cut off and disconnected from people and have trouble being around friends and family.

Who are some of the people from whom you feel disconnected?

_____

_____

_____

_____

List some of the things you have normally done that you no longer feel like doing.

_____

_____

_____

_____

What activities do you especially miss being involved in?

_____

_____

_____

_____

(Continued on the next page)

Symptoms of Abuse Scale
Profile Interpretation *(Continued)*

II. PHYSICAL SYMPTOMS

People who are experiencing extreme stress often have physical symptoms such as anxiety, panic attacks, tiredness, headaches and stomach aches.

What physical symptoms do you experience most often?

_____

_____

_____

_____

How are these physical symptoms affecting your life?

_____

_____

_____

_____

Describe what it is like to experience these symptoms?

_____

_____

_____

_____

(Continued on the next page)

Symptoms of Abuse Scale
Profile Interpretation *(Continued)*

III. COGNITIVE

People who are experiencing extreme stress often have symptoms that revolve around the recollection of the abuse. These unwanted thoughts or images about the abuse can occur while watching a certain television program, hearing a certain song, smelling a familiar fragrance, reading about something in the newspaper, or can simply happen for no reason at all.

If this has happened in the past month, describe the situation and what happened.

_____

_____

_____

_____

What situations seem to bring the flashbacks on?

_____

_____

_____

_____

How have you been coping with these thoughts?

_____

_____

_____

_____

(Continued on the next page)

Symptoms of Abuse Scale
Profile Interpretation *(Continued)*

IV. EMOTIONS

People who are experiencing extreme stress often experience symptoms that include intense feelings such as grief, depression, guilt, anger and irritability. These feelings must be overcome and controlled for you to successfully move on in life. They can keep you from reducing the stress in your life.

What feelings do you experience most intensely?

_____

_____

_____

_____

What were the triggers for your feelings?

_____

_____

_____

_____

How are you attempting to manage these strong emotions?

_____

_____

_____

_____

Exercises for Stress Reduction

Here are a variety of stress reduction exercises.
Pick and choose the ones that will work for you.

Staying in the Present

Much of the stress that you are experiencing comes from dwelling on the past or worrying about future events. To reduce and ultimately stop these thoughts, you need to start living in the present moment. When you do this, all of your attention becomes focused on what you are currently doing. When this happens, all worries, fears and desires cease to enter your consciousness. As you begin to focus your attention, you will notice that thoughts of the past and future will arise. When they do, note it and gently turn your awareness back to the present.

Experiential Exercise – Staying in the Present

Try the following exercise to see how easy it is for you to relax. Sit still for several minutes and try to quiet your logical mind. Close your eyes and stop the internal chatter going on in your mind. Let go or block out any interfering thoughts, anxieties or emotions that pop into your head. Try not to think about the past or the future. Simply concentrate on your breath.

Exercise

Exercise is another excellent method for combating and managing stress and relieving some of the physical symptoms you may be experiencing. In our society, the time needed to exercise is often very hard to find, but it is very important that you put aside time each week in order to exercise your body and relieve tension. Several different types of exercises are available for you to use in reducing stress:

Aerobic Exercise uses sustained, rhythmic activity involving primarily the large muscles in your legs. Aerobic exercises include such activities as jogging, running, brisk walking, swimming, bicycling, kickboxing or other high intensity martial arts and aerobic training. The goal of aerobic exercise is to gradually increase your stamina and enhance your cardiovascular system.

Low Intensity Exercise is used to increase muscle strength, enhance flexibility and quiet your mind. Low intensity exercises include slow walking, light gardening, yoga, walking in the woods, calisthenics and *soft* martial arts like Tai Chi.

Affirmations

When thoughts about past abuse begin to pop into your head, one of the best tools for quieting your mind is affirmations. Affirmations are phrases you can use to reprogram your mind. They are brief statements that put you in the proper frame of mind to accept intuitive inputs. Affirmations are a way of sending your brain a message that the desired result has already been achieved.

What you state, in the present tense, can easily be achieved.

Examples of affirmations that might be helpful are:

"I am focusing on healing."

"I am learning how I want to be treated."

"I will not let the abuse take over my life."

"I have learned so much about myself."

"I like myself and deserve to be treated well."

Experiential Exercise — Affirmations

Using the examples of affirmations above, formulate some of your own affirmations below:

1) _____

2) _____

3) _____

4) _____

Practice your affirmations on a daily basis. Select one of the affirmations that you feel comfortable with and repeat the affirmation for about five minutes each day for one week.

Listen to Music

Listening to music is probably one of the easiest forms of relaxation. To benefit from the relaxation of music, you should select music that is soothing and that you find peaceful. To benefit the most from your music relaxation sessions, you should find approximately one-half hour of uninterrupted time by yourself daily.

Visualization

Visualization, also called *guided imagery*, can be used to reduce mental activity and manage stress. This method is used to induce deep relaxation and relieve tension. This can be read aloud to participants in a group.

Experiential Exercises — Visualization

Close your eyes and imagine yourself walking with a safe person through the forest.

You can hear the wind swishing through the trees as you walk and feel the wind gently touching your face.

You can hear birds singing and see the deep blue sky above the trees.

As you continue walking you find a small patch of grass alongside a beautiful lake.

You walk toward the lake and find yourself in the middle of a small patch of grass.

It is very quiet here, the water is perfectly calm and the grass feels soft below your feet.

You lie down on the grass so that you can feel the sun on your face.

You are completely relaxed, at peace with yourself and the world.

It is quiet and you feel yourself drifting off to sleep.

Allow your mind to take in the smells and sounds of this relaxing place.

Thought Stopping

Whenever you notice an anxiety-producing thought about the abuse entering your stream-of-consciousness, internally shout the word **STOP** to yourself.

Experiential Exercise — Thought Stopping

Close your eyes and imagine a situation in which a stressful thought often occurs. This might be a situation like talking in front of a group of people you do not know, going on a date or going to a meeting at work. About thirty seconds after you begin to think about the situation, shout **STOP** as the thought begins to enter your consciousness. Eventually, with some practice, you will be able to imagine hearing the word **STOP** shouted inside your head.

Breathing

Because breath is vital to life itself, proper breathing is very important and can even be an excellent form of stress reduction. The pace at which you breathe and the depth of your breathing are vital in relaxation and stress reduction.

When you encounter stressful situations, your breathing quickens and becomes more shallow. Breathing can also help to relax and quiet your body.

Diaphragmatic breathing (often called belly-breathing), in which you take in long, very deep breaths, is an especially powerful tool for relaxation. In diaphragmatic breathing, you push out your stomach and draw in a long deep breath. Then you exhale as slowly and as long as possible.

Repeat this until relaxation occurs.

Experiential Exercise — Breathing

- Pay attention to your breathing.

- Don't try to change it, but just become more aware of it. This will allow you to easily be brought into conscious awareness.

- Make note of the parts of your body or ways your mind is attempting to interfere with the natural movement of your breathing.

- If your attention wanders and takes you away from the focus on your breathing, simply bring back your attention so that you return to your focus.

- Dwell on the rise and fall of your chest as you inhale and exhale.

- Simply allow your attention to settle you and stop distracting thoughts.

Progressive Relaxation

Progressive relaxation helps you to bring relaxation to all parts of your body through concentrated awareness. It allows you to actually produce relaxation by focusing self-suggestions of warmth and relaxation in specific muscle groups throughout the body.

Experiential Exercise — Progressive Relaxation

Sit in a comfortable position. Close your eyes and start to feel your body relaxing. Think of yourself as a rag doll. Let the relaxation pass through each organ and body part you have. In this exercise, start with your feet and progressively relax all the parts of your body. This will help you to manage your stress effectively. Begin by having your body progressively relax with such statements as:

"I am relaxing my feet . . . . My feet are warm . . . . . .My feet are relaxed."

"I am relaxing my ankle . . . . My ankles are warm . . . .My ankles are relaxed."

"I am relaxing my calves . . . . . . My calves are warm. . . . .My calves are relaxed."

"I am relaxing my knees. . . . . . . My knees are warm . . . . .My knees are relaxed."

"I am relaxing my thighs . . . . . . My thighs are warm. . . . .My thighs are relaxed."

Do this with the rest of your body until you are totally relaxed from your head to your feet. Block any distractions out of your mind as you concentrate on relaxing your entire body.

Meditation

Meditation is the practice of attempting to focus your attention on one thing at a time. It is a method in which you use repeated mental focus to quiet your mind, which in turn quiets your body.

In meditation, focusing on one thing allows your mind to stay concentrated and excludes all other thoughts. There are many different forms of meditation.

In meditation you can focus by repeating a word like *"OM,"* count your breaths by saying *"one, two, three"* after you exhale with each breath, or gaze at an object like a candle or a piece of wood without thinking about it in words.

Nutrition

Many people admit that during high stress periods they eat more than usual and eat less healthy foods. A poor diet contributes negatively to your reactions to stress and stressful situations.

Although there is no best diet for every person, following are some general guidelines to help you eat healthier at all times:

- Reduce the fat in your diet
- Eat a balanced diet with sufficient calories, vitamins and minerals.
- Do not eat excessive amounts.
- Reduce cholesterol consumption
- Increase consumption of protein sources such as fish, poultry, nuts, lean meats and low fat dairy products
- Eat foods low in sodium
- Eat fewer foods with high amounts of refined sugar
- Avoid excessive alcohol consumption
- Eat plenty of fruits and vegetables
- Be aware of how stress affects your personal eating habits
- Limit amounts of caffeine

Engage in Simple Pleasures

Sometimes small, simple pleasures can help you to reduce the stress associated with extreme stress. These simple pleasures could include things like going to see a movie, calling friends to get together for dinner, taking a walk, playing with your dog or cat, and sitting on your back porch.

Learn?

What did you learn about yourself?

_____

_____

_____

_____

_____

_____

_____

_____

_____

_____

_____

_____

_____

_____

_____

_____

_____

_____

_____

_____

_____

_____

_____

Work On?

What do you want to work on the most?

_____

_____

_____

_____

_____

_____

_____

_____

_____

_____

_____

_____

_____

_____

_____

_____

_____

_____

_____

_____

_____

_____

_____

_____

_____

Stress Management Plan?

How would you describe your stress management plan?

_____

_____

_____

_____

_____

_____

_____

_____

_____

_____

_____

_____

_____

_____

_____

_____

_____

_____

_____

_____

_____

_____

_____

_____

Some Long-Term Effects of Abuse

- Self-neglect or self-injury

- Eating disorders

- Suicide attempts

- Chronic pain

- Depression, anxiety, panic attacks

- Sleep disorders

- Sexual dysfunction

- Aggression towards others

- Substance abuse

Fears in Leaving an Abusive Situation

- Retaliation from the abuser

- Having no place to go

- Having no money

- Losing custody of children

- Immigration status being reported

- Religious beliefs

- Cultural beliefs

SECTION II:
Types of Abuse Scale

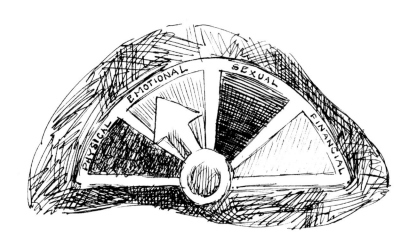

Name_____

Date_____

Types of Abuse Scale Directions

Domestic violence is not limited to physical abuse. It is also not limited to a partner. It could be a family member, friend, or co-worker. There are many different forms of abuse including physical, verbal, emotional, sexual and financial abuse. In addition, most victims of abuse often experience it in more than one of these ways at the same time. The Types of Abuse Scale can help you identify the different ways that you may be the victim of abuse.

This assessment contains 40 statements. Read each of the statements and decide if the statement is true or false. If it is true, circle the word **True** next to the statement. If the statement is false, circle the word **False** next to the statement. Ignore the numbers after the True and False choices. They are for scoring purposes and will be used later. Complete all 40 items before going back to score this scale.

In the following example, the circled False indicates that the item is **False** for the participant completing the TYPES of ABUSE SCALE.

This person . . .

1. Pushes, shoves, slaps, punches and / or bites me   True (1)   (False (0))   Score _____

This is not a test and there are no right or wrong answers. Do not spend too much time thinking about your answers. Your initial response will be the most true for you. Be sure to respond to every statement.

(Turn to the next page and begin)

Types of Abuse Scale

This person . . .

1. Pushes, shoves, slaps, punches, and/or bites me   True (1)   False (0)   Score _____

2. Exhibits extremely jealousy   True (1)   False (0)   Score _____

3. Keeps me from spending time with family and friends   True (1)   False (0)   Score _____

4. Throws objects at me   True (1)   False (0)   Score _____

5. Locks me out of the house   True (1)   False (0)   Score _____

6. Abandons me in dangerous situations   True (1)   False (0)   Score _____

7. Ties me up   True (1)   False (0)   Score _____

8. Threatens me   True (1)   False (0)   Score _____

9. Requires me to get permission before doing things   True (1)   False (0)   Score _____

10. Does not help me when I am sick or disabled   True (1)   False (0)   Score _____

TOTAL _____

This person . . .

11. Ignores my feelings   True (1)   False (0)   Score _____

12. Ridicules me   True (1)   False (0)   Score _____

13. Insults my gender   True (1)   False (0)   Score _____

14. Belittles my values and beliefs   True (1)   False (0)   Score _____

15. Disapproves constantly of what I do   True (1)   False (0)   Score _____

16. Criticizes me without ever complimenting me   True (1)   False (0)   Score _____

17. Makes all of the important decisions   True (1)   False (0)   Score _____

18. Threatens regularly to leave me   True (1)   False (0)   Score _____

19. Refuses to allow me to work   True (1)   False (0)   Score _____

20. Abuses pets and other animals   True (1)   False (0)   Score _____

TOTAL _____

(Continued on the next page)

(Types of Abuse Scale, continued)

This person . . .

21. Treats me as a sex object   True (1)   False (0)   Score _____

22. Makes me wear sexual clothing against my will   True (1)   False (0)   Score _____

23. Criticizes me sexually   True (1)   False (0)   Score _____

24. Touches me when or where I do not want to be touched   True (1)   False (0)   Score _____

25. Withholds sex and/or affection   True (1)   False (0)   Score _____

26. Calls me names during sex   True (1)   False (0)   Score _____

27. Shows sexual interest in others in public   True (1)   False (0)   Score _____

28. Has had affairs with other people   True (1)   False (0)   Score _____

29. Forces me to have sex   True (1)   False (0)   Score _____

30. Commits sadistic sexual acts   True (1)   False (0)   Score _____

TOTAL _____

This person . . .

31. Does not help to support me or my family financially   True (1)   False (0)   Score _____

32. Uses me for my money   True (1)   False (0)   Score _____

33. Denies me access to financial information   True (1)   False (0)   Score _____

34. Does not allow me to earn my own money   True (1)   False (0)   Score _____

35. Gives me an allowance   True (1)   False (0)   Score _____

36. Takes and spends any money I earn   True (1)   False (0)   Score _____

37. Does my banking, even though I want to   True (1)   False (0)   Score _____

38. Asks me to justify all of my purchases   True (1)   False (0)   Score _____

39. Controls my income and/or assets   True (1)   False (0)   Score _____

40. Denies me money for necessities   True (1)   False (0)   Score _____

TOTAL _____

(Go to the Scoring Directions on the next page)

Types of Abuse Scale Scoring Directions

The Types of Abuse Scale is designed to help you to explore the different ways that you may be experiencing abuse. To score this scale, you need to determine your scores on each of the individual scales and for the overall Types of Abuse total.

To score the Types of Abuse Scale:

Look at the 40 items you just completed. Now you need to focus on numbers after each choice rather than the **True** or **False**. Total your score for each section.

Use the spaces below to transfer your scores to each of the scales below.

PHYSICAL/PSYCHOLOGICAL ABUSE SCALE: Total Score from #1 through #10   = _____

VERBAL/EMOTIONAL ABUSE SCALE: Total Score from #11 through #20 = _____

SEXUAL ABUSE SCALE: Total Score from #21 through #30 = _____

FINANCIAL ABUSE SCALE: Total Score from #31 through #40 = _____

Add together all of the totals from the individual scales to find your Abuse Total and write that number in the blank below:

ABUSE TOTAL _____

The Profile Interpretation section on the next page can help you interpret your scores.

Types of Abuse Scale

Profile Interpretation

INDIVIDUAL SCALE SCORE	TOTAL FOR ALL FOUR SCORES	RESULT	INDICATIONS
0 to 1	0 to 9	very low/none	You are experiencing very little or no abuse at this time.
2 to 4	10 to 19	low	You are experiencing some abuse at this time.
5 to 7	20 to 29	moderate	You are experiencing a moderate amount of abuse at this time.
8 to 10	30 to 40	high	You are experiencing a great deal of abuse at this time.

The higher your score on the Types of Partner Abuse Scale, the more you might be experiencing that type of abuse.

In the areas in which you score in the **Moderate** or **High** range, make efforts to ensure that you are safe and have a plan prepared to escape the violence if necessary.

No matter if you scored **Low**, **Moderate** or **High**, the exercises and activities that follow are designed to help you to develop a comprehensive plan for ensuring the safety of you and your family.

(Continued on the next page)

Types of Abuse Scale
Profile Interpretation (Continued)

PHYSICAL / PSYCHOLOGICAL ABUSE

People scoring high on this scale are currently exposed to physical and psychological abuse. Physical violence is the intentional use of physical force. Sometimes it can cause injury, disability or even death, but physical violence does not have to cause physical injury in order to be abuse. Physical abuse can include any form of unwanted physical contact, such as hitting, burning, biting, shoving, throwing, punching, kicking, restraining, or threat with a weapon. Psychological abuse can include threats of physical violence or any behaviors that cause you to feel less independent.

VERBAL / EMOTIONAL ABUSE

People scoring high on this scale are currently exposed to verbal and emotional violence. Verbal / Emotional violence can include verbal threats of physical violence, humiliation, name-calling, continual blaming, withholding information, doing things to make the victim feel embarrassed, and isolating a person from family and friends.

SEXUAL ABUSE

People scoring high on this scale are currently exposed to someone who uses physical force to coerce them to engage in sexual intercourse or sexual acts against their will. Sexual abuse can include pursuing sexual activity when you are not fully conscious, when you are not asked for consent, have said "no," or are afraid to say "no."

FINANCIAL ABUSE

People scoring high on this scale are currently exposed to financial or economic abuse. The abuser has control over your money and other economic resources. Financial abuse includes putting you on an allowance, withholding money or credit cards, making you account for every penny spent, forcing you to beg for money, preventing you from working or from finishing or obtaining education, and/or misusing shared resources.

Safety Plan #1 — Things to Do to Be Safe

Your safety (and that of your children and/or loved ones) is the most important thing. Below are listed some of the things you can do to ensure your safety.

CONTACTS	PHONE NUMBERS
Local Police Department	
Domestic Violence Hotlines	
Domestic Violence Shelter	
Friends	
Relatives	

There is always the danger with written safety plans that the abuser will find it.

Keep the safety plan, along with copies of important documents someplace other than home for safe-keeping, i.e., a locked drawer at work, trusted relative, friend or neighbor.

Safety Plan #2 —
Supportive Neighbors and Friends

Are there any neighbors or friends you could tell about the abuse? If so, they could call the police if they heard any violence or anger coming from your household.

NEIGHBORS OR FRIENDS	PHONE NUMBERS

There is always the danger with written safety plans that the abuser will find it.

Keep the safety plan, along with copies of important documents someplace other than home for safe-keeping, i.e., a locked drawer at work, trusted relative, friend or neighbor.

Safety Plan #3 — Leaving Your Home Safely

Do you know how to get away to a safe place? Write about how you would get yourself (and your children) away if you needed, in an emergency.

_____

_____

_____

_____

_____

List three places you could go if you leave.

1) _____

2) _____

3) _____

Are there weapons where you live? Think about how you could get rid of them.

_____

_____

_____

_____

There is always the danger with written safety plans that the abuser will find it.

Keep the safety plan, along with copies of important documents someplace other than home for safe-keeping, i.e., a locked drawer at work, trusted relative, friend or neighbor.

Safety Plan #4 — What Would You Take?

What would you take with you if you had to leave?

Place a check mark by those people / items in this list.

❑ Children

❑ Family Members

❑ Other people

❑ Money

❑ Keys to your car

❑ Keys to your house

❑ Medicine

❑ Important papers (birth certificates, immigration & status documents, visa, etc.)

❑ Social Security Cards

❑ Driver's License

❑ Bankbook

❑ Credit Cards

❑ Passports

❑ Insurance papers

❑ Items for your children

❑ Jewelry

❑ Welfare paperwork

❑ School records

❑ Medical records

❑ Mortgage payment book

❑ Other _____

❑ Other _____

There is always the danger with written safety plans that the abuser will find it.

Keep the safety plan, along with copies of important documents someplace other than home for safe-keeping, i.e., a locked drawer at work, trusted relative, friend or neighbor.

Safety Plan #5 — Children

How could you take your children away safely?

_____

_____

_____

_____

List any potential dangers to your life or the children's lives if you do this.

_____

_____

_____

_____

What can you do, or will you do to protect your children?

_____

_____

_____

_____

There is always the danger with written safety plans that the abuser will find it.

Keep the safety plan, along with copies of important documents someplace other than home for safe-keeping, i.e., a locked drawer at work, trusted relative, friend or neighbor.

Safety Plan #6 — Supportive People

Are there any neighbors or friends you could tell about the abuse? If so, they could call the police if they heard any violence or anger coming from your household.

PERSON	HOW THEY COULD HELP YOU

What could you do to protect your pets?

_____

_____

_____

_____

_____

 **There is always the danger with written safety plans that the abuser will find it.**

Keep the safety plan, along with copies of important documents someplace other than home for safe-keeping, i.e., a locked drawer at work, trusted relative, friend or neighbor.

Safety Plan #7 — Your Safety

If you have left your abuser, get a PPO (Personal Protection Order) from the court.

How would you go about this?

_____

_____

_____

Where would you go to do so?

_____

_____

_____

Have you given a copy of the PPO to:

The police and other authorities ?	Yes	No
People who care for your children?	Yes	No
People at the children's school?	Yes	No
Your supervisor at work?	Yes	No

Have you:

Changed the locks on your doors?	Yes	No
Do you have a security system?	Yes	No
Do you have outside lights?	Yes	No
Do you have smoke alarms?	Yes	No
Do you have a pet for protection?	Yes	No

There is always the danger with written safety plans that the abuser will find it.

Keep the safety plan, along with copies of important documents someplace other than home for safe-keeping, i.e., a locked drawer at work, trusted relative, friend or neighbor.

Safety Plan #8 — Other Ways to Protect Yourself (and Children)

In the spaces to the right, write about how you will keep yourself (and your children) safe.

Information I still need to add to my safety plan.	
Who are the people who care for your children? They should be warned about the only ones who are allowed to pick up your children.	
Where is the telephone number for the domestic violence hotline?	
Who can you talk to for emotional support? What are their telephone number(s)?	
What are other important telephone numbers that you might need?	

There is always the danger with written safety plans that the abuser will find it.

Keep the safety plan, along with copies of important documents someplace other than home for safe-keeping, i.e., a locked drawer at work, trusted relative, friend or neighbor.

Safety Plan #9 — My Plan

In the lines below, describe your comprehensive plan for escape of an abusive situation.

_____

_____

_____

_____

_____

_____

_____

_____

_____

_____

_____

_____

_____

_____

_____

_____

_____

_____

_____

 **There is always the danger with written safety plans that the abuser will find it.**

Keep the safety plan, along with copies of important documents someplace other than home for safe-keeping, i.e., a locked drawer at work, trusted relative, friend or neighbor.

Safety Plan #10 — Safety of My Children

What types of things can you do to ensure the safety of your children?

_____

_____

_____

_____

_____

_____

_____

_____

_____

_____

_____

_____

_____

_____

_____

_____

_____

_____

_____

_____

_____

_____

There is always the danger with written safety plans that the abuser will find it.

Keep the safety plan, along with copies of important documents someplace other than home for safe-keeping, i.e., a locked drawer at work, trusted relative, friend or neighbor.

Severe Abuse

What would you describe as the most severe type of abuse you are experiencing?

_____

_____

_____

_____

_____

_____

_____

_____

_____

_____

_____

How does the person abusing you explain or justify this?

_____

_____

_____

_____

_____

_____

_____

_____

_____

_____

_____

_____

Cycle of Abuse*

Tension Builds – Abuser begins to get angry and communication breaks down

Incident – Physical, sexual, emotional and/or financial abuse occurs

Make-Up – Abuser apologizes and promises it will never happen again

Calm – Abuser acts like the abuse never happened

*This cycle can happen continually
in a relationship.*

*Adapted from Lenore Walker, *The Battered Woman*. New York: Harper & Row, 1979.

Some Examples of Abuse

1) Stalking me

2) Intimidating me

3) Calling me names

4) Biting or hurting

5) Putting me down

6) Preventing me from having a job

7) Sexually assaulting me

8) Tying me up against my will

9) Preventing me from going to my place of worship

10) Consistently blaming me

SECTION III:
Partner Behavior Scale

Name_____

Date_____

Partner Behavior Scale Directions

Many men and women who have been physically or emotionally abused in the past are reluctant to get involved in new romantic relationships. This is often because they are afraid of entering another abusive relationship.

This assessment is designed to help you evaluate the behaviors of people with whom you are considering developing a romantic relationship.

It contains 28 statements divided into four specific abusive behaviors. Read each statement and decide the extent to which the statement describes you.

Circle 3 if the statement is **A lot like him or her**

Circle 2 if the statement is **A little like him or her**

Circle 1 if the statement is **Not like him or her**

In my current romantic relationship, my partner . . .

Wants to know about who I talk with   3   (2)   1

In the above statement, the circled 2 means that the assessment-taker thinks this statement is a little like his partner. Ignore the TOTAL lines below each section. They are for scoring purposes and will be used later.

This is not a test and there are no right or wrong answers. Do not spend too much time thinking about your answers. Your initial response will be the most true for you. Be sure to respond to every statement.

(Turn to the next page and begin)

Partner Behavior Scale

3 = A Lot Like Him or Her   2 = A Little Like Him or Her   1 = Not Like Him or Her

In my current romantic relationship, my partner . . .

Wants to know about who I talk with	3	2	1
Calls constantly and visits unexpectedly	3	2	1
Doesn't want me to work	3	2	1
Seems a little possessive	3	2	1
Checks on me	3	2	1
Pressures me for an exclusive commitment	3	2	1
Accuses my friends and family of being trouble makers	3	2	1

SECTION I TOTAL = _____

3 = A Lot Like Him or Her   2 = A Little Like Him or Her   1 = Not Like Him or Her

In my current romantic relationship, my partner . . .

Expects me to meet all of her or his needs	3	2	1
Does not want me to make phone calls	3	2	1
Does not like me to have my own transportation	3	2	1
Questions me when I am late getting home	3	2	1
Tells me how to dress and act	3	2	1
Insists that I ask for permission to do things I want to do	3	2	1
Controls all of the money	3	2	1

SECTION I TOTAL = _____

(Continued on the next page)

(Partner Behavior Scale, continued)

3 = A Lot Like Him or Her   2 = A Little Like Him or Her   1 = Not Like Him or Her

In my current romantic relationship, my partner . . .

Was abused as a child	3	2	1
Abuses alcohol / abuses drugs	3	2	1
Lies	3	2	1
Likes to threaten weapons	3	2	1
Has a history of cheating on partners in the past	3	2	1
Doesn't take responsibility for his or her behavior	3	2	1
Feels he or she can do anything he or she wants	3	2	1

SECTION I TOTAL = _____

3 = A Lot Like Him or Her 2 = A Little Like Him or Her   1 = Not Like Him or Her

In my current romantic relationship, my partner . . .

Physically punishes me	3	2	1
Pushes me around	3	2	1
Hits me	3	2	1
Is cruel to animals	3	2	1
Lashes out when angry	3	2	1
Gets upset and becomes physical	3	2	1
Forces me to participate sexually against my will	3	2	1

SECTION I TOTAL = _____

(Go to the Scoring Directions on the next page)

Partner Behavior Scale Scoring Directions

The Abusive Behavior Inventory is designed to help you determine if you are in a healthy relationship or in a potentially abusive relationship. Add the numbers you've circled for each of the four sections on the previous pages. Put that total on the line marked TOTAL at the end of each section.

Then, transfer your totals for each of the four sections to the lines below:

SECTION I   - **TOTAL** = _____ (Jealousy)

SECTION II - **TOTAL** = _____ (Control)

SECTION III - **TOTAL** = _____ (Lifestyle)

SECTION IV - **TOTAL** = _____ (Abusiveness)

Profile Interpretation

TOTAL INDIVIDUAL SCALE SCORES	RESULT	INDICATIONS
Scores from 17 to 21	High	Your partner shows an abusive attitude for these scales.
Scores from 12 to 16	Moderate	Your patner shows some signs of having an abusive attitude for these scales.
Scores from 7 to 11	Low	Your partner shows very few of the signs of having an abusive attitude for these scales, but this could still indicate abusive behavior. Continue to do the following exercises.

For scales which you scored in the **Moderate** or **High** range, find the descriptions on the pages that follow. Read the description and complete the exercises that are included. No matter how you scored, low, moderate or high, you will benefit from these exercises. Self-advocacy strategies are included to ensure safe, healthy relationships for you.

Partner Behavior Scale
Profile Interpretation

SCALE I — Jealousy

Abusive partners are often very possessive and controlling. They might be jealous of your relationships with other people, even your family of origin. They may want to do everything with you alone. They may want you to reduce or eliminate the time you spend with your family and friends. They may ask that you stop doing other activities that you do without them. They may even ask you to account for your whereabouts and time. They may want you to check in with them or may call you several times per day to check on you. They often question you by asking "Where were you?" They may not want you to work and/or be around other people.

How does your partner show his or her jealousy?

_____

_____

_____

_____

What activities has your partner asked you to quit? What were the reasons given?

_____

_____

_____

_____

How does your partner keep track of your whereabouts?

_____

_____

_____

_____

(Continued on the next page)

Partner Behavior Scale
Profile Interpretation *(Continued)*

SCALE II — Control

Abusive partners attempt to impose their opinions and worldview on you. They often have traditional sex-role beliefs for both men and women. They may expect you to meet their every wish and need. They may attempt to control you because they feel like you belong to them and they want to control how and with whom you spend your time. They may not want you to work and will often control all of the money in the household. They may even deprive you of having transportation or using a telephone. They may even require you to ask permission to do the things you want to do.

How does the person in your relationship try to control you?

_____

_____

_____

_____

What is the person's view of the sex roles of men and women?

_____

_____

_____

_____

In what ways does this person expect you to meet his or her wishes?

_____

_____

_____

_____

(Continued on the next page)

Partner Behavior Scale
Profile Interpretation *(Continued)*

SCALE III — Lifestyle

Abusive partners show their abusive behavior through the lifestyle they live. They often feel entitled to do whatever they want. They often have histories of heavy alcohol or drug abuse. They might have a reputation for cheating on their past partners. They often have been abused as children or exposed to domestic violence between parents and/or grandparents.

List ways the lifestyle of the person in your relationship worries you.

_____

_____

_____

_____

What do you know about this person's past relationships?

_____

_____

_____

_____

What do you know about this person's childhood?

_____

_____

_____

_____

(Continued on the next page)

Partner Behavior Scale
Profile Interpretation *(Continued)*

SCALE IV — Abusive Behavior

Abusive partners tend to be abusive to you and to others. They tend to be explosive and display a bad temper. They are often verbally abusive to other people and blame others for their own mistakes or problems. They often expect too much of children. They can be very cruel and critical of other people. They may also mistreat or torture animals and pets.

In what ways does the behavior of your partner worry you?

_____

_____

_____

_____

List the times and situations where your partner has shown a bad temper.

_____

_____

_____

_____

List the times and situations where your partner has shown physical aggressiveness.

_____

_____

_____

_____

Self-Advocacy

Self-advocacy allows you to take control of your life and take charge of your happiness in future relationships. The following exercises will help you to be in control and in charge of your life.

Putting yourself first

Self-advocates are good at putting themselves first and getting their wants and needs met. How would you begin to put yourself first?

_____

_____

_____

What needs and wants do you have that you rarely, if ever, tell people?
Who would you like to tell?

_____

_____

_____

Stand up for yourself

Self-advocates are good at standing up for themselves.
How would you begin to stand up for your rights?

_____

_____

_____

What decisions do you need to make based on what is in your best interest?

_____

_____

_____

Negatives

Self-advocates are good at dealing with negative or disrespectful comments. What negatives things have people said about you that are not true? Write about how they are not true.

_____

_____

_____

_____

_____

How do you tear yourself down? Write about the things you say about yourself?

_____

_____

_____

_____

_____

_____

_____

Now write about you, giving yourself the respect you deserve. What positive things do you deserve?

_____

_____

_____

_____

_____

_____

Helplessness

Self-advocates are good at being in control. List the times and ways you have been helpless and out of control in your relationships.

_____

_____

_____

_____

_____

_____

_____

_____

Now list what you need to do to be less helpless and more in control of your life and your happiness.

_____

_____

_____

_____

_____

_____

_____

_____

Developing Positive Connections with Other People

Many people have a hard time finding positive, healthy relationships. Many people leaving abusive relationships and entering new ones don't feel strongly connected to anyone. What are some of the ways you are currently using to meet positive new people?

Places to meet people	People I have met in these places
Support Groups	
Community Events	
Sports Events	
Artistic Events	
Special-Interest Clubs (hiking, music, etc.)	
Place of Worship / Spiritual Groups	
Other	

Healthy Relationships Worksheet

Many people who have been abused in the past find it difficult to develop and keep positive, healthy relationships. Look for relationships with these people who will support you and treat you well. They may be co-workers, friends, siblings, parents, children, boyfriends, girlfriends or other family members. In the spaces below, describe the people with whom you have healthy relationships:

Person	Relationship	Why I feel these are healthy relationships

Unhealthy Relationships Worksheet

Many people who have been abused in the past find themselves in many negative, unhealthy relationships. You might have such people around you; people who do not support you and do not treat you well. They may also be co-workers, friends, siblings, parents, children, boyfriends, girlfriends, or other family members. In the spaces below, describe the people with whom you have unhealthy relationships:

Person	Relationship	Why I feel these relationships are unhealthy

Changing Unhealthy Relationships

You have choices about how you will deal with people with whom you have unhealthy relationships. These choices will depend on your relationship with each individual and the reasons for the unhealthy relationship. People who are in physically abusive relationships, or ones with a threat of physical abuse, should never attempt to end the relationship without a safety plan in place.

Look at the Unhealthy Relationship Worksheet you just completed. On this worksheet, transfer the people listed. Then, write about the actions you can take. Refer to pages 43 – 52 of the Types of Abuse Scale to further develop your Safety Plan.

Person	Action I Will Take	When I Will Take Action

Trusting Relationships

Write about the people you know who have relationships that are intimate and trusting. What have you observed about their behaviors toward each other?

_____

_____

_____

_____

_____

_____

_____

_____

_____

_____

_____

_____

_____

_____

_____

_____

_____

_____

_____

_____

_____

_____

An Ideal Relationship

How would you describe an "ideal" intimate and trusting relationship?

_____

_____

_____

_____

_____

_____

_____

_____

_____

_____

_____

_____

_____

_____

_____

_____

_____

_____

_____

_____

_____

_____

_____

_____

_____

_____

_____

Ideal Qualities

Describe what you think would be the "ideal" qualities you would want in a partner.

_____

_____

_____

_____

_____

_____

_____

_____

_____

_____

_____

_____

_____

_____

_____

_____

_____

_____

_____

_____

_____

_____

_____

_____

_____

_____

_____

Healthy Relationships

You need people in your life . . .

. . . to whom you can tell anything.

. . . who accept you — for you.

. . . who help you to feel good about you.

. . . who will listen to you.

. . . who respect and trust you.

. . . who give you good advice.

Indicators of an Unhealthy Relationship

- Dishonesty

- Threats

- Controlling

- Abandonment

- Betrayal

- Constant criticism

- Violation of boundaries

- Lack of commitment

- Lack of caring

SECTION IV:

Elder Abuse Scale

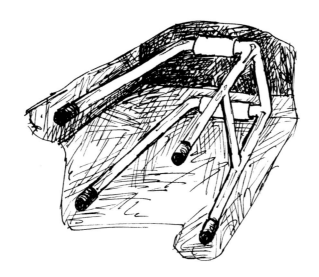

Name_____

Date_____

Elder Abuse Scale Directions

Elder abuse affects many people of all social, economic, and religious backgrounds. If you are a survivor of elder abuse you are probably still experiencing a wide variety of emotions.

This assessment can help you identify where your growth areas are in terms of your recovery. It contains 32 statements. Read each of the statements and decide how much you agree with the statement. In each of the choices listed, circle the response on the right of each statement.

In the following example, the circled "Like Me" indicates that the statement describes the person taking the assessment:

SECTION 1: SELF-ESTEEM

Talking about the abuse makes me feel worse   Not Like Me

This is not a test and there are no right or wrong answers. Do not spend too much time thinking about your answers. Your initial response will be the most true for you. Be sure to respond to every statement.

(Turn to the next page and begin)

Elder Abuse Scale

SECTION 1: SELF-ESTEEM

Talking about the abuse makes me feel worse	Like Me	Not Like Me
I worry about what other people think	Like Me	Not Like Me
I am sensitive to criticism	Like Me	Not Like Me
I feel helpless and not in control	Like Me	Not Like Me
I feel like I'm a coward	Like Me	Not Like Me
If I let myself feel my emotions, I will lose control	Like Me	Not Like Me
I see myself as a failure	Like Me	Not Like Me
I have no self-confidence	Like Me	Not Like Me

TOTAL LIKE ME _____

SECTION 2: ANXIETY

I an anxious and nervous a lot of the time	Like Me	Not Like Me
I am now afraid of being alone	Like Me	Not Like Me
I have a sense of impending doom or dread	Like Me	Not Like Me
I have sudden unexpected panic attacks	Like Me	Not Like Me
I often feel on edge	Like Me	Not Like Me
I sometimes feel like I am losing control	Like Me	Not Like Me
I am concerned about looking foolish	Like Me	Not Like Me
I feel detached from my body at times	Like Me	Not Like Me

TOTAL LIKE ME _____

(Continued on the next page)

(Elder Abuse Scale, continued)

SECTION 3: GUILT

I feel like I don't (didn't) fight hard enough	Like Me	Not Like Me
I wish I had (could have) done more to stop it	Like Me	Not Like Me
I feel that I do (did not) live up to expectations	Like Me	Not Like Me
I feel guilty because I did not press charges against my abuser	Like Me	Not Like Me
I feel foolish for trusting those who abused me	Like Me	Not Like Me
I want to harm those who abused me	Like Me	Not Like Me
I do not (did not) take suitable precautions against the abuse	Like Me	Not Like Me
I feel like the abuse is (was) my fault	Like Me	Not Like Me

TOTAL LIKE ME _____

SECTION 4: DEPRESSION

I feel sad a lot of the time	Like Me	Not Like Me
The future looks hopeless to me	Like Me	Not Like Me
I have lost interest in things that used to be important to me	Like Me	Not Like Me
I often feel worthless	Like Me	Not Like Me
I have to push myself to do things	Like Me	Not Like Me
I sometimes feel life is not worth living	Like Me	Not Like Me
I have lost my appetite or eat way too much	Like Me	Not Like Me
I want to sleep all of the time	Like Me	Not Like Me

TOTAL LIKE ME _____

(Go to the Scoring Directions on the next page)

Elder Abuse Scale Scoring Directions

People who experience elder abuse experience many different types of negative emotions. This assessment is designed to measure how well you are managing your emotions. Four of the emotions that are prominent after elder abuse make up the four scales for the assessment. To score the assessment you just completed:

1. Add the number of "Like Me" responses you circled in each of the FOUR previous sections and put the total on the line at the end of the section.

2. Then, transfer your totals for each of the three sections to the corresponding lines below:

SECTION 1: SELF-ESTEEM TOTAL   =   _____

SECTION 2: ANXIETY TOTAL   =   _____

SECTION 3: GUILT TOTAL   =   _____

SECTION 4: DEPRESSION TOTAL   =   _____

Profile Interpretation

TOTAL INDIVIDUAL SCALE SCORES	RESULT	INDICATIONS
Scores from 6 to 8	High	You are experiencing many of the emotions described on the scale.
Scores from 3 to 5	Moderate	You are experiencing some of the emotions described on the scale.
Scores from 0 to 2	Low	You are experiencing very few of the emotions described on the scale.

For scales which you scored in the **Moderate** or **High** range, find the descriptions on the pages that follow. Then, read the description and complete the exercises that are included. No matter how you scored, low, moderate or high, you will benefit from all these exercises.

Elder Abuse Scale
Descriptions

SCALE I: SELF-ESTEEM

People scoring **High** on this scale tend to have a low perception of their own self-worth as well as their perception of what others think of them. They feel inadequate a lot of the time, and generally feel inferior to other people.

SCALE II: ANXIETY

People scoring **High** on this scale tend to experience an unusual amount of anxiety and worry. They will worry or fret and feel uneasy about stress circumstances or situations in their life.

SCALE III: GUILT

People scoring **High** on this scale tend to feel guilty about the abuse that was perpetrated upon them.

SCALE IV: DEPRESSION

People scoring **High** on this scale tend to have feelings of sadness and low energy, experience loss of interest in life and life activities, have trouble getting to sleep or want to sleep all of the time, and harbor feelings of hopelessness and emptiness.

Self-Esteem Exercises

What are some of the situations in which you feel inferior?

_____

_____

_____

_____

What are the types of negative emotions you have in these situations (sad, jealous, angry, criticized, rejected)?

_____

_____

_____

_____

What are you thinking about in these situations? What are you telling yourself?

_____

_____

_____

_____

What are the consequences of your low self-esteem? How does it affect you?

_____

_____

_____

_____

Daily Feelings Log

The following log will help you to track your negative feelings, explore the thoughts that may be causing these negative feelings, and help you to replace negative thoughts with more positive ones:

Negative Feelings You Have	Thoughts That Upset You	More Positive Thoughts
Frustration	*How could my own daughter abuse me?*	*She made a mistake; she was experiencing a lot of stress in her life too.*

Anxiety Exercises

Anxiety tends to be an anticipation problem. People anticipate something that will happen in the future, anticipate that something horrible is about to happen, or anticipate being in a situation that they dread.

Complete the following exercises to help you learn to deal more effectively with your anxiety.

Anxiety is often associated with some types of fear. What fears often underlie your feelings of anxiety? (For example, "I am afraid to be reunited with my family.")

_____

_____

_____

_____

What happens when you try to suppress these feelings?

_____

_____

_____

_____

What in your life do you wish you could control, but cannot? How does this affect your anxiety?

_____

_____

_____

_____

(Continued on the next page)

(Anxiety Exercises, continued)

People with anxiety also experience a great deal of anger. Think about a time when you have felt anxious. Did you also experience anger? What else was going on that triggered your feelings of anger?

_____

_____

_____

_____

What types of things can you do or say to reduce your angry feelings?

_____

_____

_____

_____

Have you ever felt that people in your support system don't care about you or about what is going on in your life? When?

_____

_____

_____

_____

What types of things happen that you feel anxious about?

_____

_____

_____

_____

Guilt-Related Exercises

People who have experienced elder abuse often experience guilt related to these events. You may be feeling guilty about something you did or did not do, beliefs or thoughts that you had, or having certain feelings about what happened to you. It is important that you explore how you may be drawing guilt-related conclusions based on faulty thinking. Complete the following exercises to help you with this process.

Guilt is often a result of looking back at choices you have made in the past. What types of decisions have you made that you think might have been related to the abuse you suffered?

_____

_____

_____

_____

What do you feel you *"should have"* or *"could have"* done to prevent what happened?

_____

_____

_____

_____

Do you see that your *"should have"* and *"could have"* thoughts could only have happened if you were certain about what would happen? It is now time to forgive yourself. You could not see into the future.

I need to forgive myself for these thoughts:

_____

_____

_____

_____

Forgiving Yourself

It is helpful to forgive yourself in order to feel better. Are you too hard on yourself for things you have done in your life? Write about them in the blanks that follow:

Feelings associated with your guilt	I forgive myself . . .
Anger	*I forgive myself for not telling someone about the abuse earlier. I felt that I had good reasons at that time.*

Depression Exercises

In a depressed state, people tend to withdraw within themselves, continue to think about what bothers them, and focus on how bad they feel. They often think about such things as family problems, personal problems and financial problems. Emotions are never wrong. They are always present and serve as indicators of your level of well-being.

The following list of symptoms indicates depression.

Emotional: a tired, empty, sad, numb feeling in which you show no pleasure from being with enjoyable people and engaging in ordinary activities.

Behavioral: irritability, excessive complaining about small annoyances and minor problems, inability to concentrate, not wanting to get up in the morning, crying, and a slowed-down reaction to things in the environment.

Physical: loss of appetite, weight gain, insomnia, restless sleep, headache, indigestion, and abnormal heart rate.

Which of the above do you feel yourself experiencing the most?

_____

_____

_____

_____

Which of the above do you feel yourself experiencing the least?

_____

_____

_____

_____

Converting Negativity into Positive Outcomes

When you look at life through a veil of pessimism, it can be very easy to fall into a depressive state. Think about your thought process and identify some of the pessimistic thoughts that are keeping you depressed. The following table will make it easier for you to explore your negative thoughts. In the first column, list your depressive thoughts. In the second column list how you can prove the thought wrong. In the third column, list your new optimistic goal.

Depressive pessimistic thoughts	What is the proof of my strengths?	Alternative thoughts and optimistic goals	How can I meet the goal?	When will I begin?
I can't get through this.	I have gotten through things like this in the past.	I will survive this and flourish.	I will talk with people who support me.	On Tuesday.

Putting It All Together

In the spaces provided below, write about how you will enhance your self-esteem, reduce your anxiety, eliminate guilt from your life, and be more optimistic — feeling less depressed. You may write, draw, sketch or doodle in the spaces!

I will increase my self-esteem by . . .	I will lessen my guilt by . . .
I will reduce my anxiety by . . .	I will be more optimistic by . . .

How Has Abuse Affected Me?

How has the abuse affected you socially?

_____

_____

_____

_____

_____

_____

How has the abuse affected you financially?

_____

_____

_____

_____

_____

_____

How has the abuse affected you psychologically?

_____

_____

_____

_____

_____

_____

Who Supports Me?

You are not alone. List the people who can support you now.

_____

_____

_____

_____

_____

_____

_____

_____

_____

_____

_____

You are not alone. List the social agencies that can support you now.

_____

_____

_____

_____

_____

_____

_____

_____

_____

_____

My Safety Plan

Describe your safety plan to prevent the abuse from happening again.

_____

_____

_____

_____

_____

_____

_____

_____

_____

_____

_____

_____

_____

_____

_____

_____

_____

_____

_____

_____

_____

_____

_____

_____

_____

_____

Types of Elder Abuse

- Physical

- Psychological

- Financial

- Sexual

- Neglect by family and others

- Self-Neglect

- Rights Abuse

Barriers

The survivors of elder abuse face some different barriers, including the following:

- Survivors may feel social isolation

- Survivors may be dependent on abusers

- Survivors may feel guilt or shame

- Survivors may experience withdrawal and depression

SECTION V:

Self-Empowerment Scale

Name_____

Date_____

Self-Empowermnt Scale Directions

Self-empowerment is a critical aspect in overcoming abuse by your partner. Self-empowerment is about acting in your own best interest and promoting your long-term happiness. It is about overcoming the trauma of abuse and celebrating your life. The Self-Empowerment Scale was designed to help you examine if you are successfully moving on from the trauma of abuse and living the life you have always dreamed of living.

This assessment contains 40 statements related to you and your current life. Read each of the statements and decide whether or not the statement describes you. If the statement is **TRUE**, circle the number next to that item under the **TRUE** column. If the statement is **FALSE**, circle the number next to that item under the **FALSE** column.

In the following example, the circled number under **FALSE** indicates the statement is not true of the person completing the inventory.

	TRUE	FALSE
I have a general lack of self-confidence	1	(2)

This is not a test and there are no right or wrong answers. Do not spend too much time thinking about your answers. Your initial response will be the most true for you. Be sure to respond to every statement.

(Turn to the next page and begin)

Self-Empowerment Scale

	TRUE	FALSE
(A) I have a general lack of self-confidence	1	2
(A) My self-esteem is as good as most other people	2	1
(A) I feel powerless and victimized	1	2
(A) I believe all relationships are like mine	1	2
(A) I will never find another person who would love me like he/she does	1	2
(A) I have marketable skills	2	1
(A) I often feel inferior to other people	1	2
(A) I could support myself and my family	2	1
(A) I think I could never get out of an abusive relationship	1	2
(A) I am not isolated socially	2	1
(B) I could have stopped this relationship	1	2
(B) I feel guilty a lot of the time	1	2
(B) I should have known better than to stay in this relationship	1	2
(B) I could not have prevented the abuse	2	1
(B) I am not the wrong part of this relationship	2	1
(B) I say "I should have" a lot	1	2
(B) I let others allow me to feel guilty	1	2
(B) If this relationship doesn't work, it will not be all my fault	2	1
(B) I would feel like a quitter if I left this relationship	1	2
(B) I feel guilty when I think about stopping this relationship	1	2

(Continued on the next page)

(Self-Empowerment Scale, continued)

	TRUE	FALSE
(C) I have spent most of my time taking care of other people	1	2
(C) I can be assertive when I want to be	2	1
(C) I work hard to be sure that others don't get mad at me	1	2
(C) I try to anticipate and avoid disapproval	1	2
(C) I usually place others' needs above my own	1	2
(C) I am afraid to hurt the feelings of others	1	2
(C) I am not afraid to express a differing opinion	2	1
(C) I am not as assertive as I could be	1	2
(C) I have trouble telling him / her what I want	1	2
(C) I am not hesitant to tell him / her how I feel	2	1
(D) I have nothing to live for without him/her	1	2
(D) I like myself and my life	2	1
(D) I can live without this relationship	2	1
(D) I tried to stop this relationship, but always go back	1	2
(D) He / she is my life	1	2
(D) I stay in this relationship even though I know it isn't healthy	1	2
(D) He / she wants me to feel good even if I'm alone	2	1
(D) I am worth something because he / she loves me	1	2
(D) I like that he / she wants me all to himself / herself	1	2
(D) I believe it is better to stay in a bad relationship than to leave	1	2

(Go to the Scoring Directions on the next page)

Self-Empowerment Scale Scoring Directions

The Self-Empowerment Scale is designed to measure whether or not you feel empowered and are your own best self-advocate.

To get your Self-Esteem score, total the numbers that you circled for the statements marked (A) in the previous section. You will get a number from 10 to 20. Then do the same for the other three scales.

(A) – LOW SELF-ESTEEM TOTAL = _____

(B) – FEELING GUILTY TOTAL = _____

(C) – WANTS & NEEDS TOTAL = _____

(D) – EMOTIONS TOTAL = _____

To get your overall self-empowerment score, add the four scores above. Your overall score will range from 40 to 80. Put your total score in the space below:

SELF-EMPOWERMENT TOTAL = _____

Self-Empowerment Scale Profile Interpretation

INDIVIDUAL SCALE SCORES	TOTAL SCALE SCORES	RESULT	INDICATIONS
17 to 20	67 to 80	High	You are in the process of overcoming the trauma of abuse and beginning to feel empowered. A high score suggests that you tend to have high self-esteem, do not feel guilty, express your wants and needs, and are not emotionally dependent. You are your own best self-advocate.
14 to 16	54 to 66	Moderate	You have moderately overcome the trauma of abuse and you feel somewhat empowered. You have some work still to do.
10 to 13	40 to 53	Low	You have not yet overcome the trauma of abuse and are not yet empowered. A low score suggests that you may lack in self-esteem, feel guilty much of the time, have difficulty expressing your wants and needs, and are probably emotionally upset.

For scales which you scored in the **Moderate** or **Low** range, find the descriptions on the pages that follow. Then, read the description and complete the exercises that are included. No matter how you scored, low, moderate or high, you will benefit from all of these exercises.

(Continued on the next page)

Self-Empowerment Scale Descriptions

A – LOW SELF-ESTEEM

People scoring low on the Low Self-Esteem Scale have difficulty finding meaning in their lives. You often wonder why you need to get up in the morning. Because of your lack of self-esteem, you begin to spend more time alone and feel a general lack of self-esteem, self-control, and self-confidence. By virtue of withdrawing from other people, people sometimes then begin to spend more time with a potential abuser.

B – FEELING GUILTY

People scoring low on the Feeling Guilty Scale have difficulty getting rid of their guilty feelings. You may feel guilty about choices you have made in the past or feel guilty about relationships in your past. You may be feeling guilty about staying with an abuser, being in a relationship with an abuser, or not being able to sustain the relationship. The good news is that this thinking can be overcome.

C – WANTS and NEEDS

People scoring low on the Wants and Needs Scale do not place a high priority in getting their needs met. You may have difficulty expressing your feelings, wants and opinions in ways that respect the rights and opinions of others, and yet, still getting what you need. You may have a difficult time sharing information about yourself and others, and communicating what you want and need in a way that makes it easy to understand what you are trying to express.

D – EMOTIONAL

People scoring low on the Emotional Scale feel like their relationship with the abusive person is the only thing of importance in their lives. You probably take responsibility for the way the person is and the problems in your relationships. You feel like you cannot live without the person, yet you want the abuse to stop.

Self-Empowerment Scale

Regardless of your score on the assessment, the following exercises have been designed to help you learn more about empowerment in the domestic violence cycle. The exercises that follow are designed to help you capitalize on your strengths and overcome your weaknesses.

Increasing Your Self-Esteem

All people experience feelings of low self-esteem from time to time. It is normal to do so. However, if you have been abused, low self-esteem may be a constant state of mind for you. Low self-esteem sometimes comes from years of being told that you are unworthy, you never do anything right, and you are a bad person. You may even be convinced that the abuse was your fault. You may know deep inside that these things are not true, but it's hard to let go of those feelings. To increase your self-esteem, complete the following exercises:

In the spaces below, list things that help you feel like you are a good, valuable, and beautiful person.

My Self-Esteem

I am a good, valuable and beautiful person. Here are some examples:

Pride

We all need to experience a sense of pride. Similarly, all people have in their lives, things of which they can be very proud. In the spaces below, list the things in life of which you are most proud. These things can be personal achievements, accomplishments at work, accomplishments related to your family, things you do in your spare time, etc.

1. _____

2. _____

3. _____

4. _____

5. _____

6. _____

7. _____

8. _____

9. _____

10. _____

My Positive Self

What kinds of positive statements do you, or can you, make about yourself? In the spaces below list some of the things you like about yourself. Don't be modest!

My appearance is _____

_____

_____

_____

My personality is _____

_____

_____

_____

My most special attribute is _____

_____

_____

_____

I am really good at _____

_____

_____

_____

People praise me for _____

_____

_____

_____

(My Positive Self, continued)

Continue to write positive statements about yourself. In the spaces below list more of the things you like about yourself. Remember not to be modest!

At work, I am the best at _____

_____

_____

_____

In school, I am/was best at _____

_____

_____

_____

My friends say my best quality is _____

_____

_____

_____

I am respected for _____

_____

_____

_____

One of my unique personality traits is _____

_____

_____

_____

Stop Feeling Guilty

One of the primary reasons that you may be feeling guilty is that you live your life by the **woulda-shoulda-coulda syndrome**. These are things you wished you had done in the past. However, these parts of your life are over and you need to move beyond things that you should have done or could have done. Now is the time to let them go. In the spaces below, list all of the *"should haves"* and *"could haves"* that you keep telling yourself over and over even though the situations are long-gone.

Could haves	Should haves

Now that you've identified the things you say over and over, and realize that this is not helping you or getting you anywhere, it is time to let them go.

Your Wants and Needs

Assertive people are able to express their desires, needs and wants. This takes some practice. Complete the following statements.

What I Want

To assert yourself, you must know what you want in life. By establishing what it is that you really want, you will be able to assert yourself when you need to. You will know what is worth fighting for and what to simply walk away from. In each of the boxes below, list what you want in each of the categories.

From my partner	
From my children	
From my mother/father	
From my family	
From my friends	
From people in the community	

Non-Assertive Situations

It is helpful to identify those situations in which you need to be more assertive. By becoming more aware of those situations in which you are not assertive, you can practice your assertiveness training skills. For each of the situations listed below, describe how you show a lack of assertiveness.

Situations in Which I Lack Assertiveness	Why I Am Non-Assertive
Saying "No" to others	
Asking for favors	
Disagreeing with others' opinions	
Taking charge of a situation	
Social situations	
Asking for something you want	
Stating your opinion	
Asking for help	
Sexual situations	
Asking for time by yourself	
Speaking in front of groups	
Others (List Them)	

Emotional Dependence

What are the primary emotions that keep you dependent emotionally on your partner or other people?

Emotion	Why this emotion keeps me dependent
Loneliness	I'm afraid to be alone

I Do Well . . .

Write about the things you do well at school or work.

_____

_____

_____

_____

_____

_____

_____

Write about the things you do well at home.

_____

_____

_____

_____

_____

_____

_____

Write about the things you do well in leisure time.

_____

_____

_____

_____

_____

_____

_____

The Guilts

In what situations do you feel guilty, even though you know the circumstances are not your fault?

_____

_____

_____

_____

_____

_____

_____

_____

_____

_____

_____

_____

_____

_____

_____

_____

_____

_____

_____

_____

_____

_____

_____

_____

_____

_____

_____

Assertiveness

Describe the ways in which you will begin to ask people for what you need and want.

_____

_____

_____

_____

_____

_____

_____

_____

_____

_____

_____

_____

_____

_____

_____

_____

_____

_____

_____

_____

_____

_____

_____

_____

_____

_____

_____

_____

Stress

People who are, or have been, in abusive relationships often suffer from stress:

- Unwanted thoughts and images

- Distressing, repeating nightmares

- Flashbacks of the abuse

- Physical reaction when reminded of the abuse

- Intrusive memories of the abuse

- Concentration problems

- Avoidance

- Fragmentation of memories

Common Guilt Issues

- Guilt about talking back

- Guilt about role-modeling to the children

- Guilt about children seeing the abuse

- Guilt about not doing more to stop the abuse

- Guilt about leaving the household

- Guilt about staying in the household

- Guilt about problems your children are having

Whole Person Associates is the leading publisher of training resources for professionals who empower people to create and maintain healthy lifestyles. Our creative resources will help you work effectively with your clients in the areas of stress management, wellness promotion, mental health and life skills.

Please visit us at our web site: **www.wholeperson.com**. You can check out our entire line of products, place an order, request our print catalog, and sign up for our monthly special notifications.

Whole Person Associates

800-247-6789